MAD about

FOOTBALL

JUDITH HENEGHAN

WAYLAND

WAYLAND

First published in paperback in 2015
Copyright © Wayland 2015

Wayland, an imprint of
Hachette Children's Group
Part of Hodder & Stoughton
Carmelite House, 50 Victoria Embankment
London EC4Y 0DZ

Editor: Nicola Edwards
Design: Rocket Design (East Anglia) Ltd

A catalogue record for this title is available
from the British Library.
ISBN: 978 0 7502 9457 7
Library e-book ISBN: 978 0 7502 8839 2
Dewey number: 796.3'34-dc23
10 9 8 7 6 5 4 3 2 1

Printed in China

An Hachette UK company
www.hachette.co.uk
www.hachettechildrens.co.uk

The author and publisher would like to thank the following for allowing their pictures to be reproduced in this publication: Cover: all Shutterstock; p4 Shuttterstock.com/Natursports; p5 (t) AFP/Getty Images, (b) AGIF / Shutterstock.com; p6 (t) Shuttterstock.com/Shawn Pecor, (b) Getty Images, p7 (t) Clive Gifford, (b) Natursports / Shutterstock.com; p8 © Lordprice Collection / Alamy; p9 (t) muzsy / Shutterstock.com, (m) © Lee Martin / Alamy, (b) Featureflash / Shutterstock.com; p10 Shuttterstock.com/Silhouette Lover; p11 (tl) Getty Images, (tr) Shuttterstock.com/Amy Myers, (b) Natursports / Shutterstock.com; p12 (t) Getty Images, (b) Shutterstock.com/ Fotokostic; p13 (t) Getty Images, (b)Shutterstock.com/ Vlad; p14 Shuttterstock.com/Rnoid; p15 (t) Laszlo Szirtesi / Shutterstock.com, (b) Shutterstock.com/almonfoto; p16 (t) Shutterstock.com/Nebojsa Markovic ; (b) FIFA via Getty Images; p17 (t) Shuttterstock.com/ Albo, (b) AFP/Getty Images; p18 Shuttterstock.com /Stanislav Komogorov; p19 (t) Steve Bardens – The FA/The FA via Getty Images, (m) Getty Images, (b) Shutterstock.com/ Fotokostic; p20 (t) Shutterstock.com/ Fotokostic, (b) Shutterstock.com/Maxisport; p21 (t) Photo Works / Shutterstock.com, (b) Natursports / Shutterstock.com; p22 (t) Shuttterstock.com/Robert J. Beyers II, (b) muzsy / Shutterstock.com; p23 (t) Getty Images, (b) Shutterstock.com/Maxisport; p24 Shutterstock.com/bikeriderlondon; p25 (t) Shutterstock.com/mrmichaelangelo, (m) Shutterstock.com/Chen WS, (b) Natursports / Shutterstock.com; p26 (t) Natursports / Shutterstock.com, (b) Laszlo Szirtesi / Shutterstock.com; p27 (t) Shutterstock.com/Kostas Koutsaftikis, (b) AGIF / Shutterstock.com; p28 (t) Shutterstock.com/bikeriderlondon, (b)Shutterstock.com/ Fotokostic ; p29 (t) Getty Images, (b) Shuttterstock.com/Fotokostic

Every effort has been made to trace the copyright holders. We apologise in advance for any unintentional omissions and would be pleased to insert the appropriate acknowledgements in any future editions of this publication.

Contents

Football first

Football is the greatest sport on Earth. You can play it almost anywhere – all you need is a bit of space and a ball. I play for the local under-11s team and we train twice a week. When I'm not training, I kick a ball around with my friends or practise against a wall. I also watch football whenever I can, either at the club ground or on TV.

World favourite

More people play or watch football than any other sport in the world. It is played in over 200 countries, by people of every skill level, age and gender. The basics are quick and easy to learn, which may help explain its popularity. Also, you don't need expensive equipment. The game relies on the skill and judgement of players which makes it unpredictable and exciting.

Watching a club match from the stands is a thrilling experience.

The aim of the game

A football match is played between two teams of eleven players on a rectangular field with a goal at each end. The aim of the game is to score by getting the football into the other team's goal using any part of the body except the arms and hands. A match lasts 90 minutes, divided into two halves of 45 minutes each. The team that scores the most goals wins the match.

Japan wins the FIFA Women's World Cup in 2011.

THE EXPERT SAYS...

Manchester United and England footballer Wayne Rooney uses all kinds of fancy footwork to control the ball and he's also brilliant at scoring goals. He says: *"... Everything I learned was from playing as a kid on the street. After school, before school, any time really."*

CHECKLIST

Get the kit:

- ☑ Well-fitting boots with studs for grass or astro soles;
- ☑ Shin pads and knee socks;
- ☑ Loose-fitting shirt and shorts;
- ☑ Gloves if you are the goalkeeper;
- ☑ Water bottle;
- ☑ Ball!

On the ball

Kicking a football is the best feeling ever. I love it when my foot makes that connection with the ball as I shoot for a goal or send it up the field. However, most kicks aren't about force; they are about controlling the ball. I'm stronger with my right foot but I always practise passing and kicking with my left foot. To play well, you need to be able to use either.

Dribbling

When you have the ball, you are 'in possession' and your aim is to move it towards the opposing team's goal in order to shoot. But running with a ball isn't easy! If you kick it too hard, an opponent may come forward and take possession themselves. Small taps between each foot help you stay in control and on top of the ball. This is called dribbling. Professional players practise hard to increase accuracy and control.

Brazil's Lucas Moura demonstrates his dribbling skills.

Passing

Football is a team sport and players must work together to avoid the other side taking possession of the ball. If a player is under attack, he or she needs to pass it to another team member with speed and precision. Popular methods include a sidefoot pass (kicking with the inside of the foot), an outside flick (kicking with the outer edge of the foot) or a backheel pass (kicking it backwards to fool an attacker).

The sidefoot pass is the most common kind of pass. Keep your eye on the ball, swing your kicking leg forward and aim to push the inside of your foot through the middle of the football in the direction you want to send it.

top tip

Always warm up first! A gentle jog around the field and some leg stretches (as some of the Real Madrid players are doing here) will help you avoid muscle strain. Remember to drink plenty of water, too.

Game on!

Football is quite simple to learn, but every game needs some rules. Rules help to keep things fair and protect players from injury. Because the rules are the same around the world, footballers from different countries can play together, even when they don't speak the same language.

Rules

Football has been around for centuries. To begin with, there were lots of different versions. Then, about 150 years ago, people started forming clubs and playing each other. To make these games fair, the Football Association (FA) was founded, swiftly followed by the Scottish Football Association (SFA). Soon, all clubs were playing by Association rules and over the next few decades these rules turned into the modern game which is today governed by FIFA — the Federation of International Football Associations.

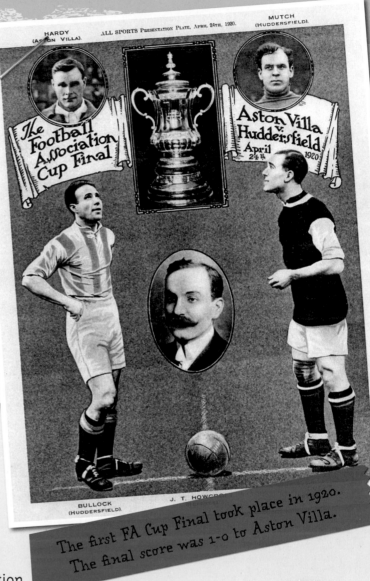

HARDY (ASTON VILLA). ALL SPORTS Presentation Plate, April 24th, 1920. MUTCH (HUDDERSFIELD).

The Football Association Cup Final

Aston Villa v. Huddersfield April 24th 1920

BULLOCK (HUDDERSFIELD). J. T. HOWCROFT

The first FA Cup Final took place in 1920. The final score was 1-0 to Aston Villa.

Always be polite to the referee – the ref's word is final!

top tip

Referees

Nowadays, every game has an independent referee who stays on the pitch and watches closely to ensure players stick to the rules. At a big game the referee might have two assistants to help keep track of the ball and the players. A match always begins with the ball at the centre point. The referee tosses a coin to see which side gets first touch of the ball before blowing a whistle to signal start of play.

Five-a-side

You don't always need teams of eleven players to enjoy a game of footie. Some people play a version called 'five-a-side' with four players plus a goalkeeper on each team. The pitch is smaller than a full-size pitch, the goals are smaller and the game time is shorter. Five-a-side is perfect for playing with friends and you can play indoors at many sports centres or outdoors on artificial grass. It has its own slightly different set of rules. Why not set up your own five-a-side team?

A game of five-a-side on artificial grass, called AstroTurf.

THE EXPERT SAYS...

Gary Lineker was famously never sent off or even cautioned by a referee in his 16-year career. He says his father was furious when he heard 14-year-old Gary swearing at the referee during a game. *"He got the coach to take me off. I learned a lesson that day."*

On the pitch

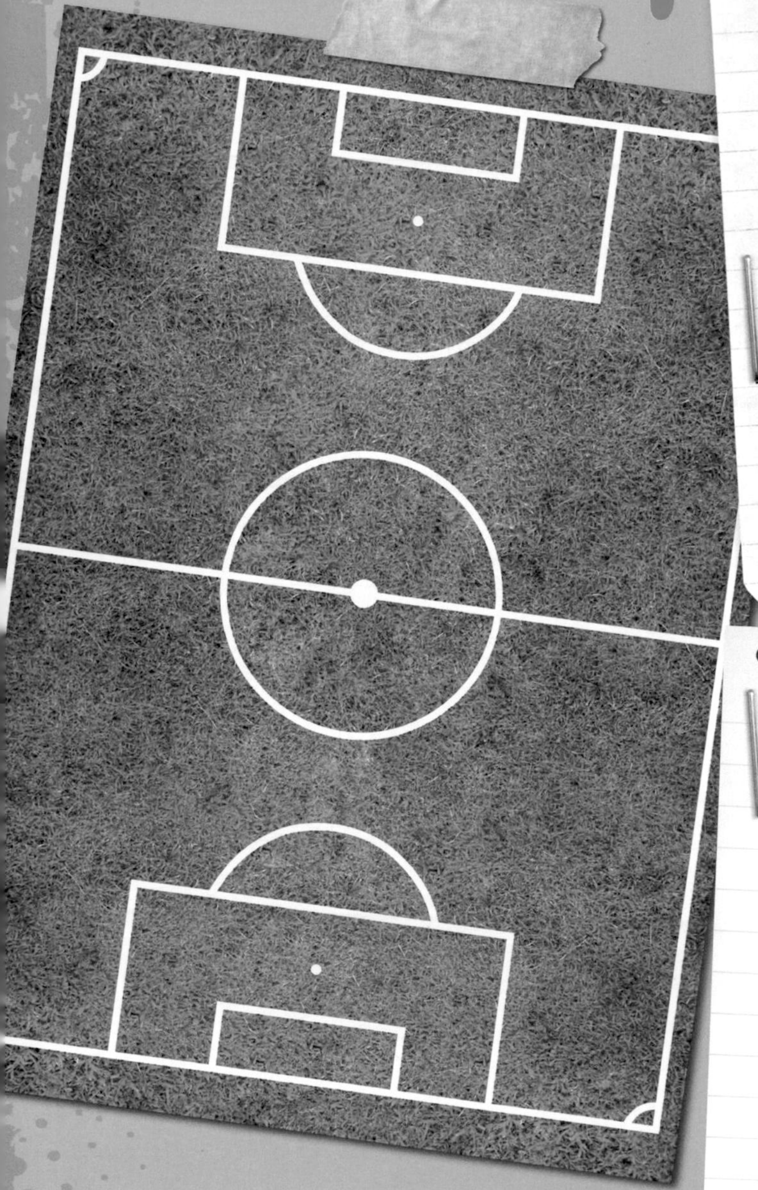

I play football with my friends in our local park all the time, but it's easier to play a match on a properly marked pitch. A football pitch has an even surface of short grass. It is a rectangular shape with lines carefully marked out to indicate touch lines, goal lines, the half-way line and the penalty area. The lines help to keep things fair!

CHECKLIST

Can you identify these areas on the diagram of the pitch?

- ☑ Centre point
- ☑ Half-way line
- ☑ Touch lines
- ☑ Goal lines
- ☑ Penalty area
- ☑ Goal area
- ☑ Penalty spot

Touch lines and goal lines

Touch lines are the two longest edges of the pitch. Goal lines are the two shorter edges. So what happens when the ball moves outside these lines?

- When a ball passes over a touch line, the team that didn't touch it last is awarded a throw-in.

- If the ball goes over a goal line and the attacking team touched it last, the defending goalkeeper is awarded a goal kick.

- If the ball goes over the goal line and the defending team touched it last, the attacking team is awarded a corner kick.

- When the whole of the ball passes over the goal line between the posts and under the crossbar without being stopped by the goalkeeper, it's a goal!

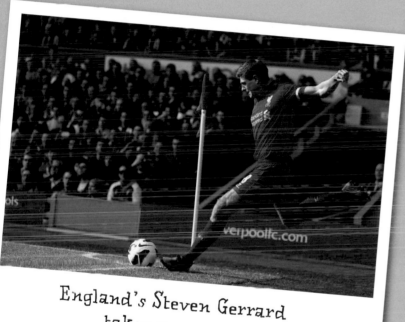

England's Steven Gerrard takes a corner.

Thiss player is taking a throw in from the touch line.

The pitch at Barcelona's Camp Nou stadium, one of the most famous football grounds in the world.

The penalty area

The penalty area is the larger of the two rectangles directly in front of the goal. The penalty spot is where the ball is placed before a penalty kick (see page 17). Goalkeepers are allowed to touch the ball with their hands anywhere inside the penalty area.

Attacking

A football team is made up of attackers, defenders and midfielders. Each player must work with the rest of the team and is equally important on the pitch. My coach usually puts me in the attack position. I've always got my sights set on scoring a goal!

David Beckham crosses the ball past the defender.

Take it forward

Attacking is about creating chances to score goals. An attacking player takes the ball towards their opponents' penalty box by dribbling the ball or passing it to other players so that they can take it forward. The opposing team's defence will try to tackle the ball away. Sometimes you have to trick your opponent by leaning or appearing to kick with one foot, when in fact you are going the other way.

Look for a space

Always look for space to run into, and think ahead while you watch what other players are doing. A team-mate may be in a better position than you, in which case try to pass the ball to them. When passing, kick the ball into the space ahead of your team-mate so that they can keep moving forward and don't have to stop to receive the ball.

top tip

It's easy to practise passes with a friend. Start by running in the same direction with about five metres between you. The player with the ball must pass it to the other player and keep running forward. The other player then passes it back, still running. In this way, the ball moves in a zig zag towards the penalty area, hopefully avoiding the other team's defence!

Players practise set-piece cross passes in training.

THE EXPERT SAYS...

Arsenal midfielder, Jack Wilshere, says: *"It's important to always try and play forwards, because that's where the goal is, but if you can't go forward, play sideways – keeping possession is the most important thing."*

Jack Wilshere keeps possession of the ball.

Defending

Although I play in an attacker position, all players in the team have to defend. I'm fast, so my job is to chase an opponent with the ball and then try to tackle it away from them. It's tricky because if I time the tackle badly I might commit a foul and then the ball goes to the other team.

Marking

Defending is about stopping the other team scoring a goal. Defenders 'mark' attackers in the other team, which means staying close to them to try to stop them receiving passes or moving towards the penalty area with the ball. Defenders will sometimes use their bodies as a shield to stop a ball getting through. However, if a player deliberately obstructs another player (rather than the ball) then this is a foul.

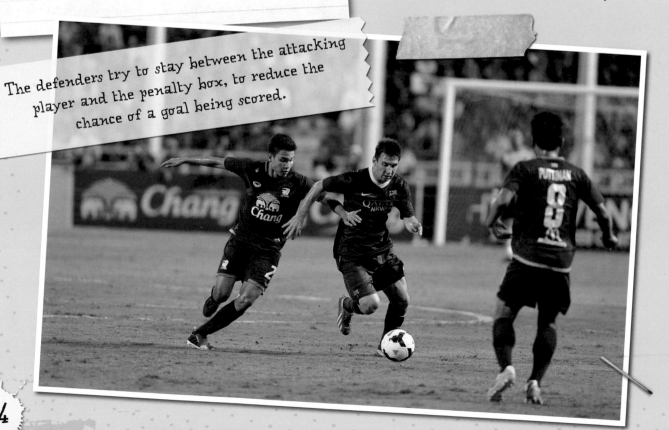

The defenders try to stay between the attacking player and the penalty box, to reduce the chance of a goal being scored.

A sliding tackle is where the defending player gets as low as possible and sticks out a leg in order to hook his or her foot around the ball. It can be highly effective, but there are risks. Time it wrong and you'll make contact with your opponent, causing a foul. You also have to get back into an upright position as quickly as possible to regain possession of the ball.

Tackling

Defenders must also look for opportunities to regain possession of the ball. They do this by intercepting passes, or by challenging an opponent for the ball. This is called tackling. Players may use a front block tackle, blocking the ball as it moves forward with the inside of their foot and kicking it away, or a side tackle, where the player hooks his foot round the side of the ball and drags it away. Make sure you kick the ball, not your opponent!

THE EXPERT SAYS...

Branislav Ivanovic (far left), who plays for Chelsea, says: "Look for your opponent's flaws. When I'm marking a player, I always try to find his weak spot – if it's his left foot, I will try to lure him on that side."

Fouls and free kicks

A great football game is fast and unpredictable, but safety must come first. The referee and assistant referees watch closely all the time to make sure that play is fair and safe. My team practises safe tackling, relying on skills rather than aggression. Our aim is to avoid injuring anyone and to avoid fouls that give the advantage to the other team.

The referee holds up a yellow card to show that a player has behaved in an unsporting or aggressive way during play.

Free kicks

A foul occurs when a player breaks a rule of the game. The most common type of foul is a tackle that is too aggressive, or where one player deliberately obstructs another. When referees see a foul, they blow their whistle to stop the game and the opposing team is usually given a free kick. This can be one of two types. A direct free kick (right) means a goal can be scored without anyone else touching the ball. An indirect free kick means one team player must touch it before another member of the same team can score a goal.

Penalty kicks

If a foul occurs inside the penalty area, a penalty kick is awarded to the fouled team. The kick is taken from the penalty spot, and no marking or tackling is allowed. A penalty kick often results in a goal being scored, so it is really important for players to avoid committing fouls inside the penalty area.

CHECKLIST

Common fouls include:

- ☑ Blocking a player so that they cannot move forward
- ☑ Pulling an opponent's shirt
- ☑ Deliberately handling the ball
- ☑ Pushing
- ☑ Tripping
- ☑ Kicking

top tip

You need to know the offside rule! A player is offside if, with the ball in play, he or she is in the other team's half of the field and nearer the other team's goal line than both the ball and the *second-last* opponent. If the referee catches a player offside, the opposing team will be given a free kick.

The player at the top is in the offside position.

Shooting

I scored my first goal for the team last week. A team-mate crossed the ball to me and I saw my chance. I aimed for the corner furthest from the goalie and remembered to kick it low and fast because high shots are easier for the goalie to intercept. I couldn't believe it when it landed in the back of the net!

Control your shot

Strikers have to make quick decisions when they see a chance to shoot. If you are close to the goal, control your shot by kicking with the inside of your foot. Sometimes you may want to swerve the ball to confuse the goalkeeper and avoid any defenders. The direction of the swerve will depend on whether you follow through across your body, or straight ahead; it takes a bit of practice to get this right. For distance shots where power is vital, kick with the top of your foot, toes pointing down. This type of kick is known as an instep drive.

CHECKLIST

Going for goal:

- ☑ Check your position
- ☑ Look for the gap
- ☑ Keep your eye on the ball
- ☑ Strike!

Heading the ball

Headers are used in defence as well as attack, but they can be particularly effective for scoring goals. An attacking player in the penalty area may jump high into the air to receive a cross before defenders can reach it. The ball makes contact with the player's forehead and is then directed downwards into the goal.

England Women's player Natasha Dowie heads the ball towards the goal.

THE EXPERT SAYS...

Demba Ba (far left), a striker for Chelsea, says: *"Have an idea of where you want to put the ball, stick to it and just focus on hitting the target."*

The young player in red takes a penalty during training.

Goalkeeping

The goalkeeper's job is to stop the ball from passing over the goal line. You need super-quick reactions in a fast-moving situation. Our goalie made a brilliant save today. He dived at full stretch across the goal mouth to deflect the ball with the tips of his fingers as it headed towards the corner.

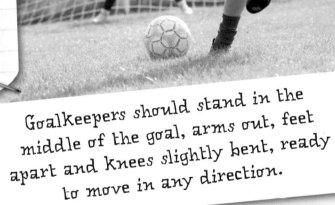

Goalkeepers should stand in the middle of the goal, arms out, feet apart and knees slightly bent, ready to move in any direction.

Blocking

A goal can come from any direction and any height. Goalkeepers need to be extra-alert and ready to spring into action. It's not all about diving though. Most goals are saved by blocking the ball with the body or catching it securely with both hands. The advantage of this kind of save is that the ball is not deflected back into the penalty box for the opposing team to take another shot.

This goalkeeper saves the ball by scooping it into his chest.

Controlling the penalty area

Goalkeepers don't just save goals. They may have to receive back passes from team-mates, kicking or heading the ball away from the goal. Also, if they catch the ball after a shooting attempt, they can throw it to a team-mate. A good goalkeeper takes charge of their penalty area and may instruct defenders.

top tip As goalkeeper you must always be on the alert, even if the ball is at the other end of the pitch. The game can change direction very quickly, or a player on the opposite team may attempt a distance shot. Be prepared!

Leading the game

Team captains shake hands before the start of a match.

Jake is the captain of our football team. This means he's our on-pitch leader. He's the most experienced player and he's really good at keeping our spirits up if the game isn't going well. He wears the captain's armband and always shows respect for the referee. The whole team thinks he does a great job.

The coach

All football teams have a coach. The coach is the team leader. He or she runs the training sessions, decides who is match-fit and discusses tactics with the players, including how many defenders and how many attackers to field during a game. The coach must also be able to motivate players both before and during a match.

Christie Rampone (far right), captain of the US women's national soccer team, is a huge inspiration. She played in her first international match in 1997 and went on to lead her team to a gold medal at the 2012 London Olympics. US coach Pia Sundhage says: "I respect her tremendously as a captain and a player. When you talk about bringing out the best performances from each player on the team, she's the one that does that."

Do your best to attend every training session. The coach is looking for commitment to the team as well as good skills and fitness.

Bayern Munich's manager Pep Guardiola celebrates a win with his team.

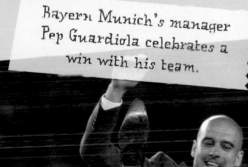

The manager

Professional teams also have a manager. The manager is like the chief coach; he or she decides which players are on the team, creates a playing strategy for each match and decides when to substitute players during play. A good manager can have a decisive influence over the team's success.

23

Support your team!

I love it when friends and family come to watch my team play. They are fantastic at cheering us on and they keep us going with drinks and snacks. Our supporters also helped us raise money to buy our team kit by organising a sponsored 'keepy-uppy'. Now we've all got a new strip with our names on our shirts.

Local level

Almost every town has its own football team. Your town may not be home to one of the major clubs but there are still plenty of reasons to watch your local team play. It's cheaper than the big league games, usually you can stand where you like, the whole family can get involved and the atmosphere is really friendly. Best of all, you'll get a great view of the action.

This youth team celebrates a win in their new strip.

The big clubs

Most football fans support one of the big clubs. Teams like Manchester United or Barcelona are known around the world and everyone has heard of their star players. These clubs get loads of news coverage, you can watch the matches at home on TV, they have huge fan clubs and supporting them is something you can talk about wherever you are. Most importantly, they play the best football. Players are signed to the team from all over the world.

Manchester United's stadium, Old Trafford.

THE EXPERT SAYS...

After Arsenal's FA Cup Final victory in 2014, Aaron Ramsey (centre) dedicated the win to the manager, Arsene Wenger, and the fans, who, he said have "always believed in us, even when things weren't going as well".

top tip

Whether you support a youth team, a local team, a professional club or your national side, being a spectator at a football match is great fun. It's also great for your team's morale.

World class

When I'm watching a Champions League match or a World Cup final I know I'm watching the world's most talented footballers at the top of their game. They have the skills, the fitness, the speed and the experience to do amazing things on the pitch. It's totally inspiring.

Lionel Messi has been voted the world's top player four times.

UEFA Champions League

The UEFA Champions League is a European club football competition that takes place every year. Big clubs from all over Europe enter knockout rounds in July. This is followed by a group stage, and the eight group winners and eight runners-up go forward to the knockout phase that ends with the final match in May. The final is one of the most watched sporting events on TV!

Chelsea win the 2012 UEFA Champions League trophy.

26

FIFA's World Cup

The world's national teams compete in the FIFA World Cup. Players set aside their usual club loyalties and instead play for their own country. The competition takes place once every four years after qualifying rounds knock out the less successful countries. The remaining countries compete in group draws in stadiums around the host country, followed by the semi-finals and the final. It is the biggest single sporting event in the world!

Germany's winning team celebrates victory over Argentina in the 2014 World Cup Final.

2014 FIFA World Cup™ Champions

CHAMPION
2014 FIFA World Cu

PELE 10

THE EXPERT SAYS...

According to Brazil's footballing legend Pelé: *"The World Cup is a very important way to measure the good players, and the great ones. It is a test of a great player."*

top tip

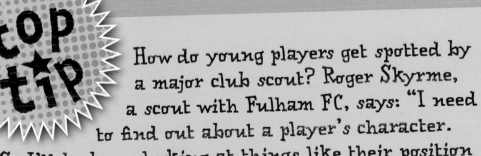

How do young players get spotted by a major club scout? Roger Skyrme, a scout with Fulham FC, says: "I need to find out about a player's character. So I'll be busy looking at things like their position on the pitch, and whether they're prepared to get stuck in and help their team-mates out. A player must have the right attitude."

The beautiful game

My friends and I support different football clubs, but we play on the same team. We spend all our time talking about football, watching football, practising and playing football! Sometimes I even dream about football. I can see why people call it 'the beautiful game'!

Keep fit and have fun on the pitch.

Good for you!

Football is good for you in all sorts of ways. It's a social game, great for making new friends. Playing improves fitness and stamina. You learn all kinds of technical skills such as marking, dodging and controlling the ball. It also helps you develop qualities such as decision-making and leadership.

In it together

In a game of football, the whole team works together to score goals and defend against the opposing side. Everyone is responsible for getting the ball down the field and into position for a striker to aim for the net. Which means that when a goal is scored, the whole team gets to celebrate!

Peter Taylor, England Under–20s head coach, has three top tips for young players:
- play as often as you can
- always go to coaching sessions and listen to your coach
- enjoy it!

THE EXPERT SAYS...

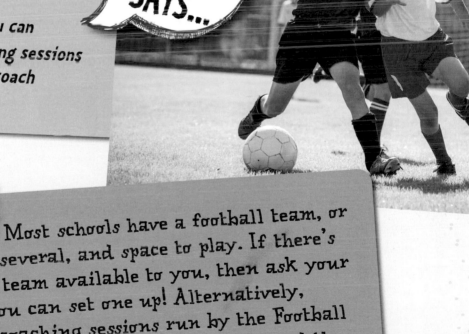

top tip

Most schools have a football team, or several, and space to play. If there's no team available to you, then ask your teachers if you can set one up! Alternatively, look out for coaching sessions run by the Football Association at FA Tesco skills centres around the country – check their website for further details.

Quiz

How mad about football are you? Try this quiz and find out!

1. What is the most important thing to do before a game?

(a) iron your kit;

(b) warm up your muscles with stretches;

(c) practise your victory dance.

2. What's the job of the captain?

(a) to motivate players and set a good example on the pitch;

(b) to score the most goals;

(c) to get first touch on the ball.

3. When is an attacking team awarded a corner kick?

(a) when a player is offside;

(b) when a player commits a foul;

(c) when the defending team kick a ball across the goal line.

4. Which of the following is a foul?

(a) blocking a player so they can't move forward;

(b) intercepting a cross;

(c) blocking the ball.

5. Why is the sidefoot pass the most common kind of pass?

(a) it helps avoid toe injury;

(b) it is the most difficult to intercept;

(c) it is the easiest to control, and the most accurate.

6. Why is it important to respect the referee?

(a) he or she might know your dad;

(b) he or she makes sure the rules are applied as fairly as possible;

(c) he or she might give you a red card if you're not careful.

7. Where is the goalkeeper allowed to touch the ball with their hands?

(a) anywhere inside the penalty area;

(b) anywhere on the pitch;

(c) anywhere inside the goal area.

8. Why is football called 'The Beautiful Game'?

(a) because a top footballer can earn a lot of money;

(b) because all the best players are good-looking;

(c) because of the skill, agility and elegance of the best players.

Answers:
1(b); 2(a); 3(c); 4(a); 5(c); 6(b); 7(a); 8(c)

Glossary

attacker A player who takes the ball forward towards the opposing team's goal.

centre point The middle of a pitch, half-way between each goal, where a match starts.

coach The team leader.

corner kick A kick from the corner of the pitch nearest the opposing team's goal.

cross A sideways pass.

defender A player who stops the ball from getting any nearer his or her team's goal.

dribbling Small taps on the ball between each foot. Dribbling allows you to move forward while maintaining possession.

FIFA The Federation of International Football Associations

five-a-side A version of football played with four players and a goalkeeper on each team.

foul An illegal action on the pitch.

free kick A kick awarded to a team after a foul has been committed. A direct free kick is straight at the goal, while an indirect free kick must be passed to a team-mate first.

goal area The smaller rectangle in front of the goal.

goal kick A kick by the goalkeeper away from the goal from inside the goal area.

goal line The two shorter edges of the pitch.

instep drive A kick using the top of the foot, toes pointing down.

intercept To take control of the ball intended for a player on the opposing team.

manager The club leader.

marking Following an opposing player closely to prevent them receiving the ball.

midfielder A player who has an attacking and a defending role.

offside An illegal position near the opposing team's goal.

penalty area The larger rectangle in front of the goal.

penalty spot The place from which a penalty kick must be taken.

possession When you have the ball.

referee An independent judge who makes sure players follow the rules on the pitch.

scout A talent-spotter for a club or team.

sidefoot pass Kicking with the inside of the foot.

sliding tackle Sticking out a leg along the ground in order to hook away the ball.

striker An attacking player in a position to score a goal.

strip Team kit, in the team's colours.

substitute A 'spare' player who can be brought on to replace an injured or tired player.

tackling Challenging an opponent for the ball.

throw in A throw from the touch line after the ball has crossed the line.

touch lines The two longest edges of the pitch.

Index